TRUTH OF LOVE

THE ORIGINAL

ARAVIND JUVVANAPUDI

People think a soul mate Is your perfect fit, and that's what everyone wants. But a true soul mate is a mirror, the person who shows you everything that is holding you back, the person who brings you to your own attention so you can change your life."

Elizabeth Gilbert.

Contents

Acknowledgements

This is the possibe way that as a human being I can tell the people what exaclty, I was aiming to tell the people in the world i've taken a lot of examples in real life situations which leads to wrong relationships and much more and aslo with the help of internet i've gathered a lot of information to explain in detail about the content in this book.

1

The story of every person.

———❤———

Every love stroy Is beautiful but our story is favorite for most of us. A cute love story begins with simple hi and ends with seven words called good bye. The gap between hi and good bye is the best memory for everyone who has gone through It.

Some people take this love to the next level and some people give up in the middle of the way, the reasons may be by their choices. But the word love deals with endless life of the two persons.

I think It's wonderful when a love story begins with a great deal of romance and affection, passion and excitement, that's how It should be. But I don't necessarily know that It's the wisest thing in the world to except that it ends there, or that it should, 30 years down the road, still look as it did on the night of your first kiss. I wondered to love someone that much? So much that you couldn't even control yourself when they came close, as if you might jjust break free of whatever was holding you and throw yourself at then with enough force to easily overheln you both.

Love is the secret behind everything love was the spaces between the stars, and fixed the ground beneath his feet.

It didn't matter if you acknowledge it or not. You couldn't stop the motion of the earth or hold back the ocean tides, or break the pull of the moon. You couldn't stop the rain or pull a shade over the sun.

Love does not come on schedule or on time It comes unexpected, it comes unplanned and finally It comes all of sudden Do not shut your doors on love just beacuse you've been hurt before. Let go of the need to be loved. Just be loving. Others will be able to see how loving and lovable you are when you express It.

The best love is unexpected. You don't just pick someone and cross your fingers it will work out. you meet them by fate and it's an instant connection, and the chemistry share is way above your heasd you just talk and notice the way their lips curve when they simle or the colour of their eyes and all the colour of their eyes and all at once know you're either lucky or served. Have you met someone that suprised you? Like you meet this person, and at first you hardly pay any attention to them. You may not even really he or she attracted to that person, but as you get to know them, you notice yourself falling for them. This person that once average to you has quickly become the greatest, most beautiful person in the world, and perhaps even the most important It's just funny looking back. You never saw something like this coming, it kind of just happened. Wait for the person that makes things feel effortless. You should not have to try so hard to keep him or her, baby girl or baby boy no matter what and you won't have to exhaust yourself with trying to make him or her stay.

Your life is nothing more than a love story. Between you and the person you love Nothing more. Every person, every experience, every gift, every loss, every pain is sent to your path for one reason and one reason only: to bring you back to Him or Her.

Each and every stage of life we walk through the path of the attraction, love at first sight, lust, and sentimental emotions. It is totally different from another side of love which we think this is the actual love. once we pass through it we will know what actual love Is.

It is a unique and passionate bond that connects you as a couple that wants the best for the other person regardless of what that means for them. It is the foundation for a healthy, loving relationship. True love is authentic and genuine.

Once buddha was asked what is difference between i like you and i love and he replied that if you like the flower you pluck it if you love the flower you pour water to it daily. day by day the meaning for the word love is updating just like the mobile network from E to 5G Didn't get It? let me go staright with this, I will divide the love into two types one is old generations love and modren generation love. The old generation love it will be very beautiful and live in another world sharing the things you have done in the whole day and promising each other caring each other but also sharing the pains and lot more when compared to modren way of love it can simply define as just the feeling that are converted to intimacy scenes that we are implementing by watching in the movies and websites.

since love is defined as very pure feeling which is converted to the lust. world is developing. out of the world population 95% of people in the world changed the feeling of love to the another side of the feeling which leads to the spending time for sometime and leaving each other. Love has a variety of feelings, emotions, and attitude. For someone love is more than just being interested physically in another one, rather it is an emotional attachment. We can say love is more of a feeling that a person feels for another person. Therefore, the basic meaning of love is to feel more than liking towards someone.

Making sacrifices is one sign of devotion to another person. When you care about someone, you have to give a little. It all comes with life. In order to receive something, one must sacrifice other things. For example, if having to make a choice between the love of your life and going to a football game, a person who is truly in love and not just in love with being in love will sacrifice the game in order to be with that person. To love another person means to feel compassionate towards them, to feel what they feel. Caring about someone and what happens to them is also a sign of love. Sharing a relationship with someone means that you have to be responsible and have to be aware that there will be times when things go wrong. Loving someone means taking these wrong things and trying to fix them.

Being in love gives a sense of completeness, makes one feel as if nothing else is needed in order to survive. Sometimes, being in love can act as a stepping stone, or a doorway into a world you never knew was out there. It can give you a new outlook on things, turn everything you've ever known into something you never thought was possible. Love can also strengthen a tie or bond that you may have with someone, in a sense that you have that much more in common.

Sacrificing anything is the greatest expression of your love. The greatest sacrifice one would have to make is death. Dying for a loved one means that your love wasn't an IT, but a THOU and dying only makes it more concrete. Trusting someone is also another important expression when it comes to love. Without trust, the love would be nonexistent, seeing as it is trust that makes people believe in each other and have faith. Without these things, the love becomes an IT relationship, not meaning much, only things.

The simplest definition of love is "a feeling of strong or constant affection for a person", but love actually has many meanings in society. For some people it is a love for someone whose important to them, for others it is how they feel towards an object or thing, or sometimes love is such a strong feeling, people become cautious towards it. Love can stay the same or it can constantly change throughout people's lives, but it plays an important role in everyday life. The theme of love is found everywhere, especially in poems. Over time different love poems explore societies and people's attitudes towards love. One poet, Sharon Olds, wrote "Sex Without Love.

Love can be defined as a sincere intense tender affection for another person. It is an expression of adoration and trust, which serves as a double-edge knife; it can be a person's strength or weakness. Despite being a basic human emotion, there is no actual way to describe love, which applies to all people. This is said because love is expressed in several different ways, and can take on numerous forms; an individual cannot decide when, how, and where love appears, as love is unpredictable.

Need of love:

We know that the desire to love and care for others is a hard-wired and deep-hearted because the fulfillment of this wish increases the happiness level. Expressing love for others benefits not just the recipient of affection, but also the person who delivers it. The need to be loved can be considered as one of our most basic and fundamental needs.

One of the forms that this need can take is contact comfort. It is the desire to be held and touched. So there are many experiments showing that babies who are not having contact comfort, especially during the first six months, grow up to be psychologically damaged. Love has a variety of feelings, emotions, and attitude. For someone love is more than just being interested physically in another one, rather it is an emotional attachment. We can say love is more of a feeling that a person feels for another person. Therefore, the basic meaning of love is to feel more than liking towards someone.

Significance of love:

Love is as critical for the mind and body of a human being as oxygen. Therefore, the more connected you are, the healthier you will be physically as well as emotionally. It is also true that the less love you have, the level of depression will be more in your life. So, we can say that love is probably the best antidepressant.

It is also a fact that the most depressed people don't love themselves and they do not feel loved by others. They also become self-focused and hence making themselves less attractive to others.

Society love:

It is a scientific fact that society functions better when there is a certain sense of community. Compassion and love are the glue for society. Hence without it, there is no feeling of togetherness for further evolution and progress. Love, compassion, trust and caring we can say that these are the building blocks of relationships and society.

Relationship:

A relationship is comprised of many things such as friendship, sexual attraction, intellectual compatibility, and finally love. Love is the binding element that keeps a relationship strong and solid. But how do you know if you are in love in true sense? Here are some symptoms that the emotion you are feeling is healthy, life-enhancing love.

Love for money:

Love should be given more importance than money as love is always everlasting. Money is important to live, but having a true companion you can always trust should come before that. If you love each other, you will both work hard to help each other live an amazing life together.

2
Infatuation

———♡———

Love is an extension of one's mind and experiences. Love sees through the little things such as race, religion, or appearance to what defines us all. Love feeds the soul joy when it finds what it wonders so seamlessly for. We are affected in many circumstances by its power everyday. In the small things such as holding open a door for another or hugging a mother, and also situations where a father holds his child in his arms for the first time. Love happens to be seen before feelings such as lust, joy, and satisfaction.

They feel very different from one another but often get labeled incorrectly. Infatuation often has only to do with what one sees on the outside and not what something truly is. Infatuation almost pulls you towards someone, making good judgement and reasoning nearly impossible. Infatuation can be caused by love at first. It is the feeling of lust that drives the mind without logical thinking. It is the body taking action before the brain can take control of the situation. Humans have to deal with this often. Seeing a crush walk into the classroom can give that person a feeling of nervousness and priority. In most cases, this instant love does not last.

It may be a few days, weeks, or months, but eventually that person will get over themselves. They will come to their senses and uncover what truly made them have that feeling that was so irresistible and undeniable. The secrets to why the feelings for that person existed come forth and are able to be seen. Previous reasons that were hidden by a cloak of invisibility are unmasked. True love can not be found through a quick glimpse at someone. It takes much more. The learning of the person's personality and character traits can lead on to a much greater feeling of love. Knowing that the person is just right takes more time than can be in any given moment. Even throughout partnership and marriage, new traits are learned.

Love is almost like a superhero and infatuation is like a sidekick. Love is powerful and overwhelming, it can go through anything and still stand strong. Infatuation has all the same qualities, though it is weaker. Infatuation can not go through test and trials that love can and survive. The main thing that differentiate infatuation and love is that infatuation is a short-lived passion for someone while love is a strong emotion formed for someone that lasts the test of time. The reason why the two are so commonly confused is because infatuation is a powerful feeling that can make you think you are in love. There are many reasons for why people mistaken being in love with someone when they are really only infatuated. One of them are because people rush into relationships without getting to know the person on a deep level. There is two sides to each human and when first meeting someone, you will usually get the good side first. When people who are infatuated rush into relationships blinded with only the good, positive things they love about that person. The "love" change once they meet the other side, the flawed side, at that point the live turns to hate almost instantly. Maybe not even hate, you can simply just become unattracted to that type of person after a while. You no longer are blinded by the good things you loved about them. The love one receive when meeting "the one" is breathtaking and instantly changes everything. For many, including myself, love is so blind it....but I can't help falling in love with you". I am wondering, did Elvis Presley really know what he was talking about when he composed that classic love song? "Love." Everyone has felt it before, right? But how do we know that emotion we feel is really the one we think we feel. Do we really know what we feel? Do we really understand the difference between love and infatuation? "I love you" is a very common phrase used by people to express their feelings to someone. It is often said by a boy to a girl because she is beautiful or similarly by a girl to a boy because he is handsome. However, their expression of words mostly does not reflect their actual feelings because they misperceive their infatuation for a particular person with love. This happens because many people have misconception about love and infatuation. Although there are few similarities between them but they are different in many other ways. Love and infatuation can be compared and contrasted on the basis of their roots, motivated feelings and affects on the relationship. Love is a tender, passionate affection for another person. On the other hand, infatuation is a foolish and extravagant passion. Though these formal definitions may show a stark contrast in meaning, discerning the difference in a real life scenario is truly no easy task. Infatuation has the eyes of a falcon. It has scores points for detail and seeks out the most fashionably impressive individual: The most beautiful girl, cutest guy and so.

Young men's love then lies not truly in their hearts,but in their eyes." Friar Lawrence lectured Romeo in the world renown play The Tragedy of Romeo and Juliet, written by William Shakespeare . Many people thought Romeo and Juliet were the extreme example of true love, but these teenagers were just infatuated. Infatuation occurs to everyone,but mostly affects adolescents. It causes people to act upon emotions and not think logically. William Shakespeare, believing infatuation was true love , gave many examples of infatuation in the play. Romeo and Juliet were infatuated as proven by Friar Lawrence's lectures, Romeo's comments, and Juliet's remarks. Friar Lawrence's lectures proved Romeo and Juliet were infatuated. When Romeo told the Friar that he forgot about Rosaline, the Friar yelled, " What a deal of brine Hath washed thy sallow cheeks for Rosaline !" The Friar evinces the audience that Romeo *acts upon his emotions because he quickly became besotted with Juliet, and he paid no attention to Rosaline, even though he cried for months because she did not return his affections. When Romeo was exiled he wished for his own death , the Friar reminded him," Thy Juliet is alive, For whose dear sake thou wast but lately dead." Romeo was acting without thought and did not think about the grief he would cause Juliet if he killed himself. When the Friar also gave advice to Juliet when she threatened to kill herself because she had to marry Paris, the Friar stated, "Then is it likely thou wilt undertake a thing like death to chide away this shame." The Friar scolded Juliet for not part in her responsibilities.

Have you ever felt butterflies in your stomach, goose bumps all over your body, and rainbows in your mind when you saw a certain person? Many people misinterpret these emotions to be the true love. And in search of it, they set themselves up for disappointments, heart-aches, and tragic miscalculations because they lack understanding of what love is in reality. These sensations are most often confused, being in essence symptoms of infatuation, which, according to the dictionary, is "the act of inspiring a foolish short-lived extravagant passion or admiration." Meanwhile at the same time, love is defined as "a profound feeling of tender, passionate constant affection for a person.

It occurs almost instantaneously, being weakened by the passing of years. Infatuation is a static process characterized by an unrealistic expectation of blissful passion without positive growth and development. Characterized by a lack of trust, lack of loyalty, lack of reciprocity, it does not pass the test of time. According to science, infatuation does not last long because it is caused by a chemical reaction in a body. "The combination between dopamine and nor-epinephrine, sometimes named the "cocktail of love", is the reason why we feel happy and see the world in a "pink color". In truth, the symptoms are the same as of a drug addiction – sleeplessness, loss of a sense of time, absolute irrational behavior." This short-lived hormonal activity causes the adrenalin to shoot up in the system. It's like building a castle on a bad foundation.Infatuation or being smitten is the state of being carried away by an unreasoned passion, usually towards another person for whom one has developed strong romantic feelings. Psychologist Frank D. Cox says that infatuation can be distinguished from romantic love only when looking back on a particular case of being attracted to a person. Infatuation may also develop into a mature love. Goldstein and Brandon describe infatuation as the first stage of a relationship before developing into a mature intimacy.Whereas love is "a warm attachment, enthusiasm, or devotion to another person", infatuation is "a feeling of foolish or obsessively strong love for, admiration for, or interest in someone or something", a shallower "honeymoon phase" in a relationship. Dr. Ian Kerner, a sex therapist, states that infatuation usually occurs at the start of relationships, is "...usually marked by a sense of excitement and euphoria, and it's often accompanied by lust and a feeling of newness and rapid expansion with a person". Phillips describes how the illusions of infatuations inevitably lead to disappointment when learning the truth about a lover. Adolescents often make people an object of extravagant, short-lived passion or temporary love.

Three types of infatuation have been identified by Brown: the first type is characterized by being "carried away, without insight or proper evaluative judgement, by blind desire"; the second, closely related, by being "compelled by a desire or craving over which the agent has no control" while "the agent's evaluation ... may well be sound although the craving or love remains unaffected by it"; and the third is that of "the agent who exhibits bad judgement and misvaluation for reasons such as ignorance or recklessness"

3

love and sex

———❧———

Have you ever thought, where did the concept of love and sex develop and evolve from? It is from the time of the Neanderthals that sexual status came into play. In the later world though it is very much different. Love and sex are more emotional and physical bonding of two people than it ever was before. At the same time however sex is just as much pleasure as it always was but the concept of love had arisen and made it more than just pleasure with multiple partners. Sexual intercourse had developed into something more. There was a whirlwind of emotions. For every culture, religion and part of the world though it was different. Even social class came into play as those in high societies believes and ways were much different than those in the lower classes. Europe, India and Japan during their medieval times had all developed their own sense and believes of what love and sex represented to them and their cultures. They all had their own preferences when it came to sex as well as having different ideas on how sex and love related to marriage within their culture and their society. Love and sex in these three areas was vastly different because of these cultural, spiritual, and social differences;

each one of these three societies helped develop the concept of what love and sex are seen as in today's world.

In medieval Europe the basics of love and sex were very different from the other regions, as it was based more on the concept of love than it was on the physical interactions of sexual intercourse. The high society in Europe had developed the concept of "courtly love". They believed that love was a sensation of emotions that were to be displayed not by physical intercourse.

In society for social, religious and cultural ways from the medieval times till our world today. Medieval Europe, India, and Japan have all had an impact on how we see sex and love in our society today. Each one contributing a small piece of their values and teachers whether it be spiritual or physical, about love or sex, they have all helped us shape our concept of sex and love today. Love and sex today are looked at as a bonding of two people and are intertwined with one another, there is no love without sex and no sex without love. These three cultures have showed us though how they can be separated though. They showed us how love and sex are connected but completely different. In the end they helped play a large part in developing our ideas of love and sex in our world today because of the different religious and social ideas that were brought into play.

Once you recognize love is the spirit and sex is the body in which the spirit is contained, then you are faced with the sharp question which comes first -- love or sex? This is like the proverbial chicken and egg dilemma. Darwinians would tend to put sex first because reproduction was the principal objective for the coming together of the two sexes. Looking at the adaptive imperatives it would seem more probable that sex came first. But then how did love follow? The impulses of romantic love which are often derided as bundling together of mawkish sentiments not only came in the wake of sex, but survived the onslaughts of bantering and slugging and shelling of severe critics. If love was indeed a figment, as it is made out by some, it would not have survived as a universal human emotion common to cultures across the world and so long. Love and sex may not be synonymous. Perhaps it is also true that love without sex does not create as strong a bond as sexual love. sexuality alone does not provide the mental and spiritual satisfaction that can be spawned by true love. That is why for a child the family becomes the source of unconditional love and also of an awareness of the value of love. It provides the link of the child to the external world from the moment his consciousness develops.

From the times of Ancient Greek, love was called Eros which meant sexual passion or Philla which meant deep friendship. Different cultures and civilizations have defined love and its many aspects in different ways. Fredrickson on the other hand has addressed to us that to understand love more we must get rid of all ideas we have heard since birth. Fredrickson proposes a new perspective on this feeling called love that we have so many phrase and stories to describe it. In the essay, "Selections from Love 2.0" Fredrickson states, "Just as your body was designed to extract oxygen from the earth's atmosphere and nutrients from the foods you ingest, your body was designed to love.

Love is a strong and powerful word, whether it is towards a family member or a special individual. But according to Aldous Huxley's rendition of an alternate future where there is a decline in family values and monogamous relationships. We follow the stories of Bernard Marx who is an introvert struggling to fit in the mold that is expected in the society. John the Savage who was born by accident and doesn't quite fit in the Savage civilization.

Sharon Olds is a contemporary poet and is known for writing intensely personal, emotional and political poems. "Sex Without Love" is an erotic poem that captures the beauty of having meaningless sex without love or pleasure. Sharon Olds shows the reader that the sex described in the poem is a cold and lonely act by effectively using imagery and theme, but she also puts an emotional and personal feeling in the poem.

What is love and sex all about?

When it comes to having sex, the intimacy has to do with merging your physical needs and body parts with the other partner whereas love making is more about connecting your minds and souls through the act of sexual intercourse. Sexual connection is a vital aspect of most romantic relationships, but it's not always as central as people may think. Partners have sex for self-interested reasons—it feels good and can boost self-esteem; and for relationship-focused reasons—it enhances closeness and pleases someone they love.

Is sex a big part of love?

Aside from reproduction, sex is essential for many reasons in any devoted relationship. It is ultimately all about the intimacy, pleasure, and the sexual expression. Intercourse has many positive intellectual, emotional, physical and social benefits.

Does sex make you fall in love?

It's not casual because when you have sex with somebody, and it's pleasurable, it drives up the dopamine system in the brain. That can push you over the threshold into falling in love.

Sacrificing anything is the greatest expression of your love. The greatest sacrifice one would have to make is death. Dying for a loved one means that your love wasn't an IT, but a though and dying only makes it more concrete. Trusting someone is also another important expression when it comes to love. Without trust, the love would be nonexistent, seeing as it is trust that makes people believe in each other and have faith. Without these things, the love becomes an IT relationship, not meaning much, only things.

There are some things that people go through life never examining or more clearly phrased, having never taken heed too; rather they except them as the here and now, "the norm", or never give them thought. And in the instances where they do think about them, are they doing so from the "correct perspective". In other words, people don't go through life, examining or even paying a second mind to the clothes they have on their skin, (maybe you feel them now, but you didn't realize the clothes touching your body surfaces, or how they felt, until I mentioned this). Well feeling clothes on your skin isn't exactly my point, but the point I am leading up to is that people go through life never paying...And the three sexual styles are role enactment, which is when the script sexual partners engage in are comparable to being on stage where they include apparatus such as mirrors, sex toys, lingerie, etc. on the "set" of their sexual encounters. There is also the sexual trance, style of sex, where partners become totally absorbed in the act of attaining pleasurable sex, and also the sexual style of partner engagement, where there is a prerequisite of a loving relationship, and the emphasis of this sexual style is on closeness, full body contact, kissing, etc. including intimate conversation before, during, and/or after sexual intercourse. After a thorough study, Frey and Hojjat concluded that the relationship between the various love styles and sexual styles varied by number of partners and also by gender. For example they found that eros, or passionate love was relative to role enactment in women, but not in men; while storge, or friendship love, was negatively related to role enactment for women, but not for men. And they also found that there was a negative relationship between partner engagement preferences and the number of sexual partners for men, but not for women. And after carefully correlating.

Can there be love without sex in a relationship? Can you have a intimate relationship without having sex? And would it be considered emotionally intimate? Can relationship lasts without a sex? Can two people who are in love share a full relationship without sex? Can there be a relationship without sex? YES!! And I think that is the most passionate love... there can be love in a relationship without sex, there's lots of things couple can do that will bring them closer and is not sexual, although sex is a natural expression of love in a relationship at some point. You need to be completely upfront with the guy you want a relationship with though. If he has a problem with it, then he doesn't respect what you are trying to do. They are going to...show more content...

In my opinion, I think it 's BEST to have a relationship without sex. Because sex drives fade in our later years, so you 'll need something in common or you 'll never get along! Sex is for marriage. If you are being pressured into sex, then you will regret it for the rest of your life. A relationship can last without sex if it is love for real but in most cases you want to have sex with the person you love just simply because its another form of intimacy. It depends on the persons involved and the situation you 're in. If you both can handle it and trust each other then you should be okay. It takes a great deal of courage and trust to withhold sex especially if you 're waiting for marriage. A physical relationship is an added bonus when you are in love, the sex is just better. How you know when someone truly loves you vary from person to person. No two people show there love for someone else in the same way. If a person truly loves you then he/she will be there for you emotionally before they are there for you physically. Putting too much focus on the physical aspect of love will ruin any emotional bond that you hope to develop.

Absolutely, there can be relationships without a sex. There are many ways to show your partner that you love him, it's just that sex is one of them. I personally believe that sex belongs in a marriage. The other ways I am talking about are, acts of service, words of affirmation, touching, gifts and quality time.

4
love for the family

One of the most immediate reasons familial love is so important is that family work to support one another. Having a support system is advantageous for both your physical and mental health and alongside other people in one's life, family are common additions to a person's support system. It includes respect for each other, and acceptance of everyone in the family, regardless of their views. Genuine love, care, loyalty, deep affection, and healthy attachment are family characteristics.

Is love a family value?

The meaning of family can be defined in many ways to different people. Family helps us in shaping our life and teaches us the value of love, affection, care, and truthfulness. It provides us tools and suggestions that are necessary to get achievement in life. Love is the greatest gift you can ever hope to give or receive. Love is so powerful; love can overcome so many of the difficult times that we have faced in life, and it can help to mend the most broken heart. It can even turn all of the ugliness in the world into the most beautiful portrait.

First, family love is the happiest I've ever had; where we are loved by parents, care, family happiness is the most precious thing in life, without it I cannot live and grow, for example, in the family: parents love children, sister love each other, relatives in the family also love each other. The family is a place to protect me and help me when I have a hard time and share the happiness and sadness. If my family is broken I will feel lonely and depressed but outside our family, I also have friends, but family love is always the most important. I respect what I have because there is nothing in this life more precious and nothing is perfect and...show more content...

This love is the mutual attraction between the body and formed into the two sexes; there is a spiritual mutual resonance. When love develops to a certain degree, the two sides have a desire for marriage to get a physical union and vow to live together for the rest of their lives. Love is characterized by the exclusion of others (the third person) love affection of two people must stick, must be together, and each side must unique to the other. If a relationship with many people, then it's considered being non-virtuous. Thus, friendship and love are limited. It cannot be denied, however, in the friendship with young people can also include elements of admiration and mutual respect.

I have couple of friends who loves their family most. I knew that my friend harshita pyla who loves her family the most keeping aside all the financial situations she supports the family very well with all the heartfull of effection and love and also a person who is so close to me ramya narisetty who loves her family in a unique way, may be she won't express but when time comes she will defneitly stand by them and fight for the things which she has to..

Family is a very important part of our lives. There can be nothing better than having love and support of your family. The significance of having a family is that a child can learn all his/ her values from it which reflects on his/ her character as well. In a nutshell, a family helps to build the character of a child. There is no greater wealth than having a lovely, supportive and great family. I belong to a middle-class family where there are four members in my sweet little family. My father, my mother, me and a sister after me are involved in it. My grandparents live in a nearby village. My father used to take us towards them frequently.

Love is a word that's been used in so many ways, it's nearly lost its meaning. We may say we love ice cream or skiing when what we mean is that we enjoy it. Love is of course commonly used to describe romantic or sexual feelings and behaviors in a romantic relationship. Some people believe love comes from God, or love is necessary for survival.

In the context of family love, the term refers to bonds characterized by deep affection, respect, loyalty, and healthy attachment in your heart. Family relationships are different from other types of bonds. The following characteristics of family love set it apart from other types of love relationships. Some people tattoo ink on their arms to show their love for their family, others post on their Instagram page, and some show their kids love by providing a safe place for them to live. Nothing can define how you show love other than yourself and what feels authentic to you.

You typically choose the person you want to start a family with when you're an adult. You might choose children to adopt or bring people into your family.

But children have no choice about who is in the family group. You don't get to choose your siblings, and you certainly don't get to choose your parents. Despite these limitations, family love still flourishes. It isn't always healthy love, but it is a deep connection, nonetheless. Finding the light in difficult relationships or setting hard boundaries is often also a sign of love.

You Face the Challenges of Living Together:

Privacy is limited because of your proximity. The more mature that person gets, though, the more they need to be mindful of how their behavior affects others. Their behavior might change, and they may have less capacity to manage daily living.

You Have Family Traditions:

Nearly every family has traditions. Family traditions may relate to holidays, but they can also be associated with other special days, situations, or rites of passage.

It's Unconditional Love, Healthy family love is unconditional. You might even have to remove yourself from the family situation. In a sense, they are still your family and always will be.

5

Relationship

word 'relationship' vaguely nowadays. We say that we are in a 'relationship' with, let's say, John Doe, but what is in it for that relationship? Is it a physical one, emotional one or maybe a relationship solely to prove that you've been there, done that? Teenagers are said to do reckless things, and we have to admit, sometimes, the things we do are because we succumb to peer pressure; we involve ourselves in relationships to fit in the crowd, but we forsake the core of the relationship—love. Love between two people is a shared feeling about their interest in one another. It is not about jealousy, conflict, testing, instead love is a positive feeling. It is the total surrender of your heart to another person when you have that confidence that they will treat your heart better than you will.

We throw around the word 'relationship' vaguely nowadays. We say that we are in a 'relationship' with, but what is in it for that relationship? Is it a physical one, emotional one or maybe a relationship solely to prove that you've been there, done that? Teenagers are said to do reckless things, and we have to admit, sometimes, the things we do are because we succumb to peer pressure;

we involve ourselves in relationships to fit in the crowd, but we forsake the core of the relationship—love. This is a general statement, and not all of us have motives as such when pursuing romantic relationships. But think about it, in any of our relationships –be it between friends, siblings, parents, or teachers– is love the centre of it all?

Love is a tricky thing to tackle. Sometimes, out of luck, we will find friends or have loved ones that are just so easy to love, but then again, there are also times when luck runs out, and we are placed with siblings or friends that make us wish God had given us someone else or placed us in somebody else's family. The hard part comes when we have to face the music that some situations just don't change; rather, it is our choice whether we conform to change or remain the same. As the ever wise Mahatma Gandhi once said, "Be the change that you wish to see in this world."

A person whose primary love language is Physical Touch is, not surprisingly, very touchy. Hugs, pats on the back, holding hands, and thoughtful touches on the arm, shoulder, or face—they can all be ways to show excitement, concern, care, and love. Physical presence and accessibility are crucial, while neglect or abuse can be unforgivable and destructive. Physical touch fosters a sense of security and belonging in any relationship. Physical touch is like a comfy couch that envelops you with.

Since, Love has many different meanings, it can be love between a friend or family member, it can be a mother's love for her child, a person's love for a pet. The people that say they love these things aren't wrong love is a very powerful emotion and feeling. Webster defines love as "a strong affection for another person out of kinship or personal connections (2): a sexual attraction, affection felt by lovers (3): affection stemming from admiration, or common interest." There are plenty of types of love and ways to express it. Love is the constant source of happiness and sadness. Even though I am young I have had the experience of falling in love. love in today's world there is an excerpt from the bible that says "Love never gives up. Love cares for others more than for self. Love doesn't want what it doesn't have. Love doesn't strut, doesn't have a swelled head, doesn't force itself on others, it isn't always 'me first, ' doesn't fly off the handle, doesn't keep score of the sins of others, doesn't revel when others grovel, takes pleasure in the flowering of truth, puts up with anything, trusts God always, always looks for the best, never looks back, but keeps going to the end. Love never dies which can be found in 1 Corinthians 13, The Message (The Life)." That is a very good way that I feel love should be expressed and explained.

There are so many ways that love can be defined of explained, and it is not that anyone is wrong it is just that some people need to understand that difference between the different types of love. People need to understand that love is not a word that should be thrown around lightly. It shouldn't be used as a mockery or to be a joke. It is a serious feeling and emotion that people need to understand. I have had the opportunity to experience falling in love and dealing with all the good and bad no matter the flaws or hardships. You don't have to go to fancy restaurants or spend every waking moment together to know you love someone. I met my best friend/partner/husband through mutual friends. We started out just being friends and having.

The word "relationship" is defined a particular type of connection existing between people related to or having dealing with each other. There are many times of ways to make a relationship last. According to the dictionary love is an intense feeling of deep affection. Love, trust, and communication are the three most important attributes in my eyes. Relationships between friends, family, and couples should be the lasting ones, and in this paper, I will Incorporate different theoretical perspectives , Discuss the role of social structure, government policy, and social inequality in love and romantic relationships and lastly analyze media presentations of families. First, no matter what type of relationship you are in, love is definitely an essential. There are many kinds of love, but most people seek its expression in a romantic relationship with a compatible partner. For some, romantic relationships are the most meaningful element in their lives, providing a source of an intense deep fulfillment. The ability to have a healthy, loving relationship is not innate. A great deal of evidence suggests that the ability to form a stable relationship begins in infancy, in a child 's earliest experiences with their parents who reliably meets the infant 's needs for food, care, protection, stimulation, and social contact. Those relationships are not destiny, but they appear to establish patterns of relating to others.

When discussing love, people generally think about the love between a husband and wife, or the love between a couple in a romantic partnership, and that is one type of love that I will be discussing. In addition to romantic love, there are other types of love also. There is the love we have for our children, our families, and also the love that we have for our friends. All of these types of love share some of the same attributes, however, they have differences also. In reading and researching different types of love, I have found that romantic love and friendship seem to be the most similar in nature, although they have differences, they share a lot of the same attributes. I found that friendship and romantic love tend to have more similarities than differences. In this paper I will examine romantic love and friendship. I will discuss the definitions of the two, and what elements each of these have. I will discuss the different theories of love, and I will compare and contrast the similarities and differences between romantic love and friendship. By friendship, I mean true friendship, or close friendships. I believe that true friendship is very different from causal friendships. True friendships involve a level of emotional intimacy that you do not find with causal friendships or acquaintances. If you look in the dictionary, it will define friendship as the relationship between friends, or the state of being friends. Friendship between men and women Friendships between men and women are familiar and socially recognized in all societies of the world. However, gender friendship remains a difficult and unyielding subject and its legitimacy or prohibition according to the cultures and values of peoples and their religions and intellectual systems.

Failed relationships arise due to complexities involved in interpersonal relationships and can result in varied dimensions of emotional distresses.

In this extended essay, the focus will be on failures, It has been declared that love between two opposite genders has significant effect on their psychological and physical dimensions (Ehsan et al. 2011).

The desire to achieve acceptance in relationships and to avoid rejection is widely acknowledged to be a central human motive (Maslow, 1987). Consistent with this claim, failed romantic relationships are known to diminish well-being and disrupt interpersonal functioning.

Few experiences in life are capable of producing more emotional distress, anguish, and suffering than is the dissolution of an important relationship (Simpson 1987).

A broken heart also known as a heartbreak or heartache is a term for the intense emotional and sometimes physical stress or pain one feels at experiencing great longing .

A common area for exploration in emerging adulthood is romantic relationships. The average American youth experiences their first romantic relationship during adolescence, prior to entering emerging adulthood. Oftentimes, these relationships in early adolescence last for only a few months but increase in length as they enter into later adolescence and early adulthood. Although relationships last longer in emerging adulthood.

In today's world there is a struggle between the old and the new. There are those that are strongly committed to traditional ways of living, including relationships and marriage. There are also people who want to make their own rules and rail against the thought of what is traditional.

I recently read an article which said that traditional relationships tend to last longer. Cue my mental eye roll as I prepare to be told how men being the bread winners with the little woman staying home cooking and cleaning is the key to everlasting love. But that is not quite what the article said that traditional relationships with clearly defined roles tend to last longer, and I can see how that makes sense. But I also think that a more modern relationship can also have roles within the relationship and be just as long lasting. Notice the word "lasting", not the word happiness is being used.

Traditional Relationship

There are many types of traditional relationships and home lives, but the basic traditional relationship involves a male and female with the man typically being the more dominant partner while the woman is more submissive.

In this context, submissive does not mean voiceless, but the woman will follow the man's lead and play a more supporting role in the relationship.

The traditional relationship also has more clearly defined roles for the couple. For example the man could be the sole provider or primary breadwinner. The man would also take care of home repairs, trash, and vehicle maintenance.

For the woman, she would take care of the cooking, the cleaning, and be the primary caretaker of any children. Although this type of relationship may seem antiquated and would not work for some, it works for many, and the relationships do tend to last longer.

Modren relationships

Modern relationships make their own rules. They break free of the stereotypical roles of relationships and marriage, and define their own coupledom. Just like the traditional relationships, there are many types of modern relationships. The roles are less clearly defined and each are expected to work together to get household chores done and the children taken care of equally.

In a modern relationship, the woman may be the breadwinner, and the man may play a more supporting role. While modern relationships offer equality to both partners, the undefined roles may result in frustrations and resentment as one half of the couple feels like the other is not pulling their weight.

Studies show that modern relationships do not usually last as long as traditional relationships, but why is that? I don't think it's about more morals, or good and bad people. But more perhaps that a person who sees themselves as a traditionalist is less likely to divorce than a more modern minded person is, no matter how miserable they are.

Quantity and quality are not remotely the same thing, and a longer marriage does not mean years of happiness. People stay in relationships for many reason, and love isn't actually at the top of the list.

Also I would think a person with their own income, who is financially independent, is more likely to call it quits on an unhappy relationship than one who is financially dependent.

Social media syndrome: Social media can play havoc in relationships. The secret flirting, personal messages and picture stalking just doesn't do any good for your relationship. It's all about sex: One night stands flings and sex dates have become extremely common in today's day and age. Make sure you are not in a relationship that revolves around sex. It isn't wrong to want more than physical intimacy.

And everyone know that traditional relationship is way better tha modren relationship in my opnion since the modren relationship is very disappointing rules which is not good for us as well as the person who is facing.

To be honest how long do you think the relationship lasts? According to the survey The average relationship lasts for 2 years and 9 months before coming to an end. Social media plays an important role in the demise of relationships. The younger the couple, the shorter the relationship – teenagers don't tend to form lasting relationships.

Relationships aren't just about what happens in your love life! Most important relationships do involve feelings but don't involve any romance, for example with family, friends and teachers.

As a teenager, you have more freedom than when you were younger. Adults around you are beginning to trust you to look after yourself. But with this freedom comes responsibility. You'll encounter new situations and new ideas everywhere: and love, sex and the way you relate to people can be some of the most significant.

Relationships have their ups and downs. To make them work well, good communication and respect is important. Everyone has the right to feel safe and happy. Try not to make judgements about people before you get to know them – sometimes the most rewarding relationships are with the most unexpected people!

What about romantic and sexual relationships?

It's normal to find you suddenly have strong feelings, or a crush, on someone. It's up to you whether you keep these feelings private, express them to the person directly, or speak to a friend first. Speaking your feelings aloud puts you in a vulnerable space. If your feelings aren't returned, you may feel exposed and rejected. However, if they are returned, you may find yourself in an exciting new friendship or relationship.

You may also find that someone has a crush on you but you don't feel the same about them. Try to treat this person the way you would want to be treated. Be honest and clear about your feelings.

Flirting

Sometimes we like someone instantly, and other times, we get to know them slowly. Flirting doesn't necessarily lead to dating; it's often just a way of finding out that someone likes us, or telling others that we like them. Everyone will express their feelings differently so it's important to remember that some people only give very subtle cues about how they feel.

It's also important to remember that flirting is never an open invitation for sex or unwanted advances. If you think someone is flirting, it doesn't necessarily mean they want to sleep with you and, in turn, just because you flirt with someone, it doesn't mean you owe them anything.

Cheating

Cheating is when one person in a relationship is secretly intimate with another person outside the relationship. If it's you that cheated, you need to own your actions and be clear with yourself about why you did it and how you feel. "Because I was drunk" is not a real answer. Even under the influence of alcohol, we still have the capacity to make choices. You might ask yourself:

Are you unhappy in your relationship?

Were you trying to make your partner jealous? If so, why?

Deep down do you want your partner to find out so the relationship has a reason to end?

If this is the case, maybe you need to end the relationship – the sooner the better. If you want your relationship to continue, think about why you cheated. In any case, you need to accept responsibility for your actions. If someone has cheated on you, you are probably feeling hurt and upset. If you have lost trust in the other person, you will need to ask yourself whether you want the relationship to continue.

6
Mother's love

Mother's love is the purest form of love. It cannot be compared with anything in this universe. The feeling of love that a mother has towards her children is inexpressible. Mothers always want the best for their children, and they will never compromise the quality of things they can offer to their little ones. she has the purest form of love in this World, and Mother is the greatest blessing for a child by God. As a child, it is our responsibility to value the sacrifice and efforts of our mother because all she wants is the betterment of her child. We are very fortunate to have a mother in our life, and we must respect our mother. We should give her all the happiness and love because she deserves all of that in return for her selfless love for us.

For a mother, a child always remains her baby even if he turns 60 or becomes a tycoon, a leader or a thinker. Mothers hold this strong aspect of loving their children in any phase of life or situation. This unconditional love of mothers, that makes them so special for every child. Mother love is... the deep, all-embracing, all-accepting, nourishing, nurturing, warm, safe, supportive love that soothes the places inside our hearts that feel scared and lonely.

How do mothers show their love?

Parents can still demonstrate their love with small gestures. Morin suggests parents write notes and put it in their lunch, offer praise, give high fives, and say kind things about your kids in front of other people. "Your actions speak volumes about how much you care for them," she insists ."A mother is a son's first true love. A son, especially their first son, is a mother's last true love," Washington said before pausing as he became emotional and apologized to the audience.

She is capable of forgiving any wrongdoing. Mother is the most important woman in everyone's life. A mother sacrifices her happiness for her child. No one else can care for their kids the way a Mother does.

A recent study has found that it's not the youngest child that's liked the most. It's actually the eldest! While eldest children around the world have had to be the example for their younger siblings and parents being extra strict on them, it looks like there was a good reason.

She is the most selfless person in this world who starts loving her children even before they come into this world. Nothing could be compared to a mother's love in this world as it is the purest form of love. Mother is like an angel for her child, who always loves her child and supports him/her. For every child, his mother has a special place in his heart because she is the first person the child sees after his birth. This is the reason why a child and a mother have a special bond between them. But not all people are fortunate enough to have mother love in their life due to many reasons. Those who have their mother with them must love and respect her.

Mother is the greatest gift for a child by God. It is the mother who always loves her children without expecting anything from them in return. It won't be wrong to say that women are inherently good mothers, but they realize the power of mother-love when they become a mother. A mother can do anything to protect her child, and she is the primary support of a child. She not only morally supports the child but also prepares her child to be a better person in life.

A mother plays many roles in her child's life from being her child's first friend to a mentor who always guides him/her, and she dedicatedly plays all these roles without complaining or hesitating.

Mother as a Best Friend

A mother is the first best friend of her child who instantly forms a special bond with the child just after his/her birth. She understands all the needs of her children and always tries to fulfill them. My mother is also my best friend. In fact, I can share all my secrets and desires with him. She always understands me and supports me. We play many games together, and our favorite game is Ludo. Many times she happily loses the game so I can win. She knows what I like and always makes me happy by cooking my favorite food. I am fortunate to have my mom as my best friend in my life.

Mother as a Mentor

A mother is not just a first best friend of a child but also his/her mentor who always supports and guides her children to achieve all the success in life. A great mentor is one who always teaches you what is right and what is wrong. A mentor not only supports you but also becomes strict with you when required. And we all can see these traits in our mothers.

My mother is truly my mentor as she not only guides me in every phase of my life but also supports me whenever

I need her. When I make any mistake, she becomes strict with me to make me understand my mistake. But soon she showers her love on me and always supports me in my decision. She helps me in my studies and asks me to be serious about my career. She teaches me both cultural and moral values. There cannot be a better mentor than a mother because she knows what is right for you and always prefers the best for you.

Mother as a Caretaker

No one can care for us as a mother does. She selflessly takes care of her child since the day he is born. She knows all the needs of her child and can do anything to fulfill them. She is always there for her children. Whenever we get sick or ill, It is our mother who takes care of us without concern about her health. For a mother, the well being of her children is the utmost important, and she always ensures that her children remain safe and protected wherever they are. A mother provides all the comfort to her child. It is the mother who makes the home cheerful and safe for children. She is like a superwoman who can manage both household work and her responsibilities towards her children. Talking about my mother, she is adorable and compassionate. She loves all my friends and me. Whenever I get sick, she gets concerned about me. She always takes care of my health and my needs. I love her the most and cannot imagine my life without her.

Mother as a Special Person of Our Life

After God, it is our mother who has the most special place in our hearts and our lives. Since the birth of a child, a mother forms a precious and special bond with him. Without thinking about herself, she thinks about her child and his happiness. She works day and night for her children so that she can make them happy. Motherhood is an integral part of a woman's life, and she selflessly gives her best to it. A newborn child recognizes her mother from her unique fragrance. And before we start speaking, our mother understands our needs through our actions. This is all because a mother and a child share a special bond, which cannot be described in words. All a mother wants is the betterment of her child and to achieve that, sometimes she supports her child and sometimes becomes strict with him. But her intentions are always pure and honest. She always wants the best for us, and she does everything to give us the best.

When we grow, we want to spend our lives on our terms and in doing so, many times we misunderstand our parents. We become selfish sometimes and fail to understand her love, but she never complains or demands anything from us. All she wants is some respect and love from her child, and every child must provide that to her.

This is important whether your mother is still living or not. Our relationships with our mother deeply affect us. One of the most powerful gifts we can give to our children is our own emotional health. A first step you can take on this journey is reading The Mom I Want to Be by T. Suzanne Eller. This book is designed to help you rise above your past and give your kids a great future.

A child should never feel as if they need to earn a mother's love. This will leave a void in their heart all of their life. A mom's love must be given unconditionally to establish trust and a firm foundation of emotional intimacy in a child's life. If love is withheld, a child will look for it in a million other ways. Sometimes they will search throughout their lifetime unless they come to some sort of peace with their past. The emotional foundation we give our children at home is foundational to their life. We cannot underestimate the value of the home and the power of a mother's love.

The profession of motherhood is all about influence. You and I have an incredible opportunity to influence the next generation by what we do as a mother every day. This is why intentionality is so important during the years that we raise our family. Be intentional about:

Your own healing from life's hurts.

Taking care of yourself.

Investing in your marriage.

Parenting.

Homemaking.

God has gifted us the very precious gift in the world and that is the mother's love. No words is good enough to explain the mother's love as well. It is a very touchy subject. There is no substitution for the mother's love in the entire world. It just can not be displaced by the money or any other things in the world. Mother is not just a word it is the world for us. Because, it is not easy to become a mother. Mother carries the child in her womb for the 9 months before the birth of the child and after the so much pain she gives a birth to a child. We can say that when the mother gives birth to the child then she also get the second birth herself. Because, the pain during the birth of the child is near to death. But the mother still survives from that painful situation with a bright smile. That is the only moment of our life when we cry and our mother smiles to see us. There is no doubt that mother is the real warrior. She sacrifices for ourself a lot. She does everything for us just to make ourself happy.

There is no boundaries for her love. She always loves us unconditionally. She never aspect in return. She supports us in every situation of our life. In life although we become mature and answerable yet we are the children in her eyes. She always loves us in the same way.

Everyone should respect their mothers. Because in the whole world there is no one can understand us or love us the way our mothers does. She cooks for us a very tasty food. If we felt sick then she takes care about ourselves at the whole night until we get recovered from it. She always stays very conscious about ourselves. She always try to give us the happiness. She fulfills our each and every wish without saying a single word. She does all the household works and also helps us in our studies with the same zeast and zeal. She never shows us that she get tired and all that. It is been said that the mother is the first teacher of our life who teaches us for the first time and then the other teachers comes into our life. It is believed that God can not stay with everyone that's why he has sent the mother with us. Mother is the another form of the god. No one can take place of mother. There is nothing in this whole world which can displace the mother's love. In this entire world we can buy everything by the money but not the mother's love. We should feel happy and blessed that god has gifted as such a very precious gift of the world. We should also love our mother in the same way as she does. Being a mother is one of the most important roles a woman can ever play. Mothers play a huge role in their children's lives, caring for them, loving them, teaching them, and so much more. The way a child develops can be largely attributed to the role that their parents and caregivers play in their lives.

Being a mother is one of the most important roles a woman can ever play. Mothers play a huge role in their children's lives, caring for them, loving them, teaching them, and so much more. The way a child develops can be largely attributed to the role that their parents and caregivers play in their lives.

A Mother's Unconditional Love

That old saying, "No one loves you like your mother", rings true now that I am older and have finally came to the realization that it could not be more true. She demonstrates her affection through hugs and kisses, she continuously asks how my day went, and treats me to lunch as a reward of my hard work. The amount of joy my mom shows for me is overwhelming because of the ways she expresses it. In addition to being a joyous person she is both physically and emotion. Before I was born my mom was preparing for every little thing yet to come. She had my dad, grandma, and aunt by her side to help. After a few months we lived in Hawaii until I was four. My dad used to tell me how proud my mom was of me. She was proud of this one moment when I was only three years old, because when she used to push me in the stroller through town, everyone walking by would compliment how beautiful I was. She just showered me with her joyous treatment.

Even though she's a small person she is always full of energy. She taught me to always be kind, caring, and honest and never let anyone push me around. She has helped me grow physically and intellectually. When my friends would come over she would always have a meal ready for all of us, or even when my dad comes home from work. She's the kind of mom who likes to cook, which I love. She is also the type of mom to give out hugs to all of my friends like she hasn't seen them in forever.

Something about my mom just helps me to always stay positive. Whether it's the way she lives life to the fullest, the troubles that she has gone through, or the way she bounces back from those troubles. My mom has always kept her positive act on, and I don't know how she does it. She will always be the person in the room that is the most bubbly and excited about life. She has gone through hard times, but tough hope has guided her through hard experiences with life.

My mom lost her dad when she was older, but it still had a big impact on her. I think that my grandpa's death was one of the most difficult things my mom has gone through.

My mom usually always stays positive. I can tell if my mom is not happy or is sad, usually when I ask her about her dad she answers positive. My mom always tells good stories when I ask about her dad. I always laugh when my mom tells me about my grandpa, because she always tells funny stories. I like when my mom tells stories, because I can tell that it makes her happy and it makes her smile. I never met my grandpa, but from the stories my mom has to offer, he seems like a pretty great guy. My mom used to take off of work on February sixth every year, she did that for thirteen years. As you can tell by that my grandpas death was very hard for my mom. Something we do to remember his is that, every year for his birthday, we set off a balloon at his grave, we also leave flowersthere for him. When we are there we shed tears of sadness, memories, and joy with my grandpa. My mom thinks about her dad everyday and think about the positive impact he had on her. My mom tells us stories about what her dad would do if he was still with us now. Throughout the stories my mom has told us I know many characteristics of my grandpa. My favorite stories are the ones that my mom likes the best, which are all of them. My mom has always told my sister and I if we ever want to talk to our grandpa or be with him, he is always there for us and here with us even though he isn't here. She also had bears made for us so we could be with our grandpa and act as though the bear is him. My sister and I sleep with our bears on our bed every night, this helps us sleep and get a better night's rest.

My mom is very fair in dealing with all of her children and treat all of us the same way without discriminating between us. My mom endeavor to give us similar presents so that nobody feels left out. She also makes a conscious effort to try not to lose her temper with one child more than the other. She also applies rules of discipline impartially to all of us. Yes, she knows each of her children are different and has his or her own temperament. Some of us are easy to talk to and reason with. Others can be stubborn and naughty and needs a firm hand. But no matter what my mom is always fair from disciplining to providing.

My mom is my security blanket. No matter how bad of a day she had, she will always be there to listen to me. I talk to her about everything even things that aren't always easy to talk about. My mom is always available to calm me down as well. Whenever something becomes too much for me, she is there calming down, giving me a hug and telling everything will be ok. The third reason I appreciate my mom is because she is yappy which represents the letter Y.
Yappy is another word for talkative. Why do I appreciate my yappy mom? I appreciate her being yappy simply because her yappy mouth is what made me into the woman I am today. My mom always have talk to me over and over and again rapidly about life. She made sure that I knew what was right and wrong. I have been raised to be helpful, caring and respectable due to that yappy mouth of my mom.

A hero is a person who is admired or idealized My mom has also supported me in means of my interests for a future career.for courage, outstanding achievements, or noble qualities. Most if not every person has their own hero, whether it be a celebrity, a family member, or some random person who you admire. My hero is someone who means the world to me and that is my mom. My mom is my hero, my idol, my model figure, my everything. I define my mom as a hero because she has provided me with guidance, motherly love, and has always been there for me. She has also supported me in every way possible. My mom is someone in my life that gives me a reason to live for and never give up. First of all, my mom is my hero because she has given me guidance and advice when I needed it the most.

My mom has been with me since day one and that was when I was conceived. She has dealt with all my disasters and has seen me grow up making mistakes. Yet, she manages to find it within herself to love me and always stay close to me. My mom has rare ways to show me her love. For example, she would play around with me and act like someone my age would act. It makes me laugh so badly that I can't help but let out tears of laughter. My mom always has those moments where she would try to do things to make me smile. There's also those times where she would act like the worried mother. I remember when I had gotten really sick that I couldn't eat for two days without wanting to throw up. I couldn't even hear people talk about food because it would send a wave of protesting cells in my stomach into a riot. It was a bad day and I was so hungry but the worse part was that I couldn't eat anything. My mom was so scared and worried that she turned into full protective mama bear mode

Nothing is enough when we start saying about our mothers, it wil take a long time i mean an unfinished and unending story.

Conclusion

After gathering all these information through the real time situations as well as with the help of internet. I want to tell that the life which we are living is not for making things complicated or to impress any other human being rather than our family members, As If you are the elder one make sure you should be the inspiration for your younger sibbling she/he should be the one who grown up by you the path that you choose, the path that you are walking, the path that you are went through. As an elder sibbiling you are the person who makes things easier to your brother/sister. All I wanted to tell you is the thing make your own choice and that choice should inspire a lot more people not only your family but also each and every one who you deals with.

All the best

Aravind kumar Juvvanapudi